Unlocking Online Income

A Comprehensive Guide to 20 Proven Ways to Make Money on the Internet

TABLE OF CONTENT

Introduction

Welcome to "Unlocking Online Income," your comprehensive guide to navigating the expansive and dynamic world of earning a living in the digital age. In an era defined by connectivity, the internet has transformed the way we work, opening doors to diverse opportunities and avenues for financial success. This book is your roadmap, designed to illuminate the pathways leading to online income, whether you're seeking a side hustle, a full-time career, or a means to diversify your revenue streams.

The digital landscape is a vast and ever-evolving frontier, and within its boundless expanse lie opportunities for freelancers, entrepreneurs, investors, coaches, and individuals from all walks of life. In the following chapters, we will embark on a journey that explores the multifaceted dimensions of online income, unveiling the strategies, tools, and insights that can empower you to thrive in this dynamic environment.

Our exploration begins with the gig economy, where freelancers are shaping the future of work by offering their skills and services on digital platforms. We'll delve into the intricacies of remote work, uncovering the advantages and challenges of a location-independent lifestyle. Entrepreneurs will find inspiration in the chapters dedicated to e-commerce, blogging, podcasting, and other ventures that allow for creative expression and financial success.

For those intrigued by the possibilities of financial markets, chapters on investing, trading, and domain flipping provide insights into the world of online finance. Coaches and tutors will discover strategies for building successful online practices, while language enthusiasts can explore the rewarding realm of online language tutoring.

As we navigate through the various avenues of online income, certain themes will emerge as guiding principles. Adaptability, continuous learning, and ethical practices will prove to be crucial in the ever-evolving digital landscape. Whether you're a seasoned professional or just starting, this book aims to equip you with the knowledge and tools needed to unlock the full potential of online income.

The future Is bright for those who are ready to embrace the opportunities presented by the digital age. "Unlocking Online Income" is not just a guide; it's an invitation to explore, innovate, and discover the boundless possibilities that await you in the vast and dynamic world of online income. So, let the journey begin. May your exploration be fruitful, and may the insights within these pages empower you to unlock new horizons in the pursuit of your online endeavours.

Chapter 1: The Digital Gig Economy

In the opening chapter of "Unlocking Online Income," we delve into the dynamic realm of the Digital Gig Economy. This chapter serves as a foundational exploration of the modern labour landscape, which has seen a significant shift towards flexibility, remote work, and project-based employment. Readers will gain a comprehensive understanding of the Digital Gig Economy, discovering the myriad opportunities it presents for individuals seeking to earn money online.

Understanding the Gig Economy:

The chapter commences with a thorough examination of what constitutes the gig economy. Readers will grasp the concept of short-term, freelance, and independent work that characterizes this economic model. We explore the rise of digital platforms connecting freelancers with clients, allowing for a borderless and diverse workforce.

Freelancing Platforms and Opportunities:

Aspiring freelancers and individuals looking to dip their toes into the gig economy will find this section invaluable. The chapter provides insights into prominent freelancing platforms such as Upwork, Fiverr, and Freelancer, offering a step-by-step guide on how to create compelling profiles, bid on projects, and establish a strong online presence. Real-world success stories and practical tips from experienced freelancers enrich the narrative, providing inspiration and guidance.

Building a Successful Freelance Career:

Transitioning from traditional employment to a freelance career can be a daunting task. This section offers a roadmap for building a successful freelance career, covering essential topics such as setting competitive rates, managing time effectively, and cultivating a diverse skill set. Strategies for client communication, project delivery, and building a reliable client base are explored, empowering readers to navigate the intricacies of freelancing with confidence.

Throughout the chapter, emphasis is placed on the benefits and challenges of participating in the Digital Gig Economy. Readers will gain a nuanced understanding of the autonomy, flexibility, and potential for financial growth that freelancing affords, balanced with insights into the competitive nature of the gig economy and the importance of continuous skill development.

By the end of Chapter 1, readers will have a solid foundation in the Digital Gig Economy, equipped with the knowledge and tools necessary to embark on their online income journey. The chapter sets the stage for the subsequent exploration of diverse online income streams, showcasing the vast opportunities available in the digital landscape.

Chapter 2: Blogging for Profit

Welcome to the world of digital expression and income generation—Chapter 2 of "Unlocking Online Income" explores the fascinating realm of "Blogging for Profit." In this chapter, readers will uncover the art and science of transforming their passion for writing into a lucrative online venture, creating a pathway to financial freedom through the power of the written word.

Creating a Profitable Blog:

The journey begins with an in-depth exploration of the key elements involved in creating a blog that not only captivates audiences but also generates income. From selecting a niche that aligns with personal interests and market demand to choosing the right blogging platform, readers will gain valuable insights into the foundational steps necessary for launching a successful blog. Practical advice on designing an aesthetically pleasing and user-friendly website lays the groundwork for an engaging online presence.

Monetization Strategies:

Building on the foundation of a well-established blog, this section delves into various monetization strategies available to bloggers. Readers will explore traditional methods such as display advertising and sponsored content, as well as more innovative approaches like affiliate marketing and selling digital products. Actionable tips on optimizing ad placements, creating compelling sponsored content, and strategically integrating affiliate links empower bloggers to turn their passion into profit.

Content Creation and Audience Engagement:

The heart of any successful blog lies in its content and the ability to engage a loyal audience. This section provides practical guidance on content creation, offering tips on developing a consistent posting schedule, crafting compelling and shareable articles, and leveraging multimedia elements to enhance reader engagement. Strategies for building and nurturing an active community through comments, social media, and email lists are explored, ensuring sustained growth and monetization potential.

Throughout the chapter, real-world case studies and success stories from accomplished bloggers serve as both inspiration and practical guidance. Readers will gain an understanding of the dedication required to build a profitable blog while learning how to navigate challenges and setbacks effectively.

By the conclusion of Chapter 2, readers will possess a comprehensive understanding of the blogging landscape and be equipped with the tools needed to embark on their journey towards blogging for profit. This chapter serves as a stepping stone for those seeking not only to share their thoughts with the world but also to turn their passion into a sustainable source of online income.

Chapter 3: Affiliate Marketing Mastery

Dive into the lucrative world of online partnerships and revenue generation in Chapter 3 of "Unlocking Online Income" as we explore "Affiliate Marketing Mastery." This chapter unravels the secrets of affiliate marketing, offering readers a comprehensive guide on how to harness the power of strategic partnerships to create a sustainable income stream.

Introduction to Affiliate Marketing:

The journey begins with a thorough introduction to affiliate marketing, unravelling the fundamental concepts and dynamics that underpin this powerful online business model. Readers will gain a clear understanding of how affiliate marketing operates, with merchants and affiliates collaborating for mutual benefit. The chapter highlights the versatility of affiliate marketing across diverse industries, making it accessible to a wide range of interests and niches.

Choosing Profitable Affiliate Programs:

Building on the foundation of affiliate marketing knowledge, this section provides practical insights into selecting the right affiliate programs. Readers will learn how to identify programs that align with their niche, offer competitive commissions, and provide valuable resources for successful promotion. Emphasis is placed on researching and vetting affiliate programs to ensure authenticity and reliability, setting the stage for a fruitful and trustworthy partnership.

Building Effective Affiliate Marketing Strategies:

Successfully navigating the affiliate marketing landscape requires more than just signing up for programs. In this section, readers will discover proven strategies for optimizing their affiliate marketing efforts. From creating compelling and persuasive content to mastering the art of strategic promotion through various channels, the chapter equips aspiring affiliate marketers with the tools they need to maximize their earning potential. Real-world case studies illustrate successful implementations of affiliate marketing strategies, offering practical insights and inspiration.

The chapter also explores the ethical considerations of affiliate marketing, emphasizing the importance of transparency and authenticity in promoting products or services. Readers will learn how to strike a balance between promoting affiliate products effectively and maintaining the trust of their audience.

By the conclusion of Chapter 3, readers will possess a solid foundation in affiliate marketing, capable of strategically selecting programs, implementing effective promotional techniques, and building a sustainable income stream. This chapter serves as a gateway for individuals seeking to leverage the power of affiliate marketing on their journey toward financial independence through online endeavours.

Chapter 4: E-commerce Ventures

Embark on a journey into the world of digital storefronts and entrepreneurial possibilities with Chapter 4 of "Unlocking Online Income" — "E-commerce Ventures." This chapter serves as a comprehensive guide for readers interested in creating and managing their online stores, exploring various models such as dropshipping, print on demand, and traditional e-commerce, while providing the tools needed to navigate the competitive landscape of online retail.

Setting Up an Online Store:

The chapter opens by guiding readers through the fundamental steps of establishing a successful online store. From choosing the right e-commerce platform to designing a user-friendly and visually appealing website, readers will gain practical insights into creating a digital storefront that not only showcases products effectively but also enhances the overall shopping experience for customers.

Dropshipping, Print on Demand, and Other E-commerce Models:

E-commerce has evolved beyond traditional inventory management, and this section delves into alternative models like dropshipping and print on demand. Readers will discover the mechanics of dropshipping, where products are sourced directly from suppliers, and print on demand, where items are created as orders are placed. This exploration offers a nuanced understanding of the diverse e-commerce landscape, allowing entrepreneurs to choose models that align with their business goals and resources.

Marketing and Growing Your Online Store:

No successful e-commerce venture is complete without a robust marketing strategy. This section provides a comprehensive overview of digital marketing tactics specifically tailored to online stores. From search engine optimization (SEO) to social media advertising, readers will learn how to drive traffic to their stores and convert visitors into customers. Practical tips on building customer trust, utilizing email marketing, and implementing loyalty programs contribute to a well-rounded approach for sustainable growth.

Throughout the chapter, real-world case studies highlight the success stories of e-commerce entrepreneurs who have navigated challenges and found prosperity in the online retail landscape. From identifying niche markets to leveraging the power of compelling product descriptions and visuals, readers will glean valuable insights from those who have successfully forged their paths in the e-commerce world.

By the end of Chapter 4, readers will be well-versed in the intricacies of e-commerce, equipped with the knowledge and strategies needed to establish and grow a successful online store. This chapter serves as a roadmap for aspiring online retailers, guiding them toward financial independence through strategic e-commerce ventures.

Chapter 5: Online Courses and E-learning

Embark on a transformative journey into the realm of digital education with Chapter 5 of "Unlocking Online Income" — "Online Courses and E-learning." This chapter serves as a comprehensive guide for individuals keen on sharing their expertise or acquiring new skills while harnessing the immense potential of online courses for income generation.

Creating and Selling Online Courses:

The chapter begins by exploring the steps involved in creating and structuring high-quality online courses. Readers will gain insights into selecting course topics, planning engaging content, and choosing the right platform for course delivery. The importance of clear learning objectives, interactive elements, and effective communication is emphasized, providing a blueprint for creating courses that resonate with learners.

Platforms for Course Creation:

Dive into a detailed examination of popular platforms for hosting and selling online courses. Whether considering established platforms like Udemy, Coursera, or exploring independent options like Teachable and Thankful, readers will discover the pros and cons of each, helping them make informed decisions based on their goals, target audience, and desired level of control over course content and pricing.

Marketing Your Educational Content:

Crafting a stellar course is just the beginning; effective marketing is crucial for attracting students. This section delves into proven strategies for marketing online courses, covering elements such as social media promotion, email marketing, and search engine optimization (SEO). Additionally, readers will explore the power of free content, webinars, and partnerships to increase course visibility and drive enrolment.

The chapter also addresses considerations like pricing strategies, course updates, and maintaining engagement with learners. Real-world examples of successful online course creators provide inspiration and practical insights into building a thriving e-learning business.

Navigating Challenges and Adapting to Trends:

As the e-learning landscape evolves, it brings both opportunities and challenges. Readers will explore potential obstacles such as competition, changing technology, and evolving learner expectations. The chapter provides guidance on staying current with industry trends, adapting to technological advancements, and continuously enhancing the learning experience to meet the needs of a diverse and dynamic audience.

By the conclusion of Chapter 5, readers will be well-versed in the art of creating, marketing, and profiting from online courses. Armed with practical strategies and a deep understanding of the e-learning landscape, individuals aspiring to enter the world of online education will be equipped to turn their knowledge into a rewarding and sustainable online income stream.

Chapter 6: Social Media Monetization

Enter the captivating world of social media and discover the art of turning your online presence into a revenue-generating powerhouse with Chapter 6 of "Unlocking Online Income" — "Social Media Monetization." This chapter is a comprehensive guide for individuals eager to leverage the vast audiences on platforms like Facebook, Instagram, Twitter, and more, transforming their social media activities into profitable ventures.

Leveraging Social Media Platforms for Income:

The chapter opens by exploring the expansive landscape of social media and the myriad opportunities it presents for income generation. Readers will gain a deep understanding of the diverse platforms available, each offering unique features and monetization methods. From content creation to community building, social media becomes a dynamic space where creativity meets entrepreneurship.

Influencer Marketing:

Delve into the lucrative realm of influencer marketing, where individuals with significant social media followings partner with brands for promotional activities. This section provides insights into building and nurturing an authentic personal brand, attracting brands and businesses for collaboration, and negotiating fair compensation. Readers will learn the nuances of becoming a trusted influencer in their niche, creating a symbiotic relationship with their audience and partner brands.

Sponsored Content and Brand Partnerships:

Explore the intricacies of sponsored content and brand partnerships, uncovering the strategies behind successfully integrating promotional materials into your social media presence. This section provides guidance on choosing the right partnerships, negotiating terms, and maintaining authenticity while promoting products or services. Real-world examples showcase how influencers and content creators have turned sponsored content into a reliable source of income.

The chapter emphasizes the importance of audience engagement, consistency, and transparency in building a successful social media monetization strategy. It also covers the significance of selecting the right platforms based on audience demographics, content type, and brand alignment.

Monetizing Across Platforms:

Different social media platforms offer distinct opportunities for monetization. This section explores monetization options on popular platforms, such as Facebook, Instagram, YouTube, and TikTok. Readers will gain insights into ad revenue, creator funds, merchandise sales, and other income streams specific to each platform. Practical tips on optimizing content for maximum reach and engagement further enhance the reader's ability to monetize effectively across diverse social media channels.

Navigating the Evolving Landscape:

The final part of the chapter addresses the ever-evolving nature of social media and the importance of adapting to changes. From algorithm updates to emerging trends, readers will gain strategies for staying relevant and maintaining a competitive edge in the fast-paced world of social media.

By the end of Chapter 6, readers will possess a comprehensive understanding of social media monetization, equipped with the tools needed to transform their online presence into a sustainable and lucrative source of income. Whether aspiring to be a social media influencer, content creator, or brand collaborator, this chapter provides the insights and strategies necessary for success in the dynamic realm of social media monetization.

Chapter 7: Stock Photography and Videography

Uncover the fascinating realm where creativity meets commerce in Chapter 7 of "Unlocking Online Income" — "Stock Photography and Videography." This chapter serves as a comprehensive guide for individuals with an eye for visual storytelling, exploring the methods and strategies to transform your passion for photography and videography into a lucrative online income.

Selling Photos and Videos Online:

The chapter begins with an exploration of the foundations of stock photography and videography. Readers will gain insights into the dynamics of licensing visual content for commercial use and discover the diverse platforms available for showcasing and selling their work. From stunning landscapes to lifestyle images, the potential for monetizing visual artistry is vast.

Building a Portfolio and Maximizing Sales:

Creating a successful stock portfolio requires more than just uploading images. This section provides practical guidance on curating a portfolio that resonates with potential buyers. Readers will learn strategies for identifying market trends, keyword optimization, and presenting their work in a way that maximizes visibility and sales. Real-world examples showcase how photographers and videographers have crafted portfolios that attract a global audience.

Licensing and Copyright Considerations:

Understanding the legal aspects of stock photography and videography is paramount. This section delves into licensing models, copyright considerations, and the importance of protecting intellectual property. Readers will gain insights into the various licensing options, from royalty-free to exclusive licenses, and learn how to navigate copyright issues in the competitive world of stock media.

The chapter also addresses ethical considerations, encouraging contributors to maintain transparency about image manipulation, provide accurate information about the context of their visuals, and respect cultural sensitivities.

Staying Competitive in a Crowded Market:

Stock photography and videography are highly competitive fields, and this section offers strategies for staying competitive and relevant. From embracing emerging visual trends to diversifying content types, readers will discover how to adapt to changes in the market and maintain a competitive edge. Tips on optimizing metadata, participating in stock photography communities, and building a personal brand as a visual content creator contribute to long-term success.

Tools and Resources for Visual Creators:

Explore the tools and resources available to streamline the process of creating and selling stock visuals. From editing software to keyword research tools, this section provides recommendations to enhance efficiency and productivity. Readers will also gain insights into the importance of investing in high-quality equipment and staying informed about industry advancements.

By the conclusion of Chapter 7, readers will be well-equipped to embark on their journey in the world of stock photography and videography. Whether pursuing this path as a hobbyist looking to monetize a passion or a professional seeking to diversify income streams, this chapter offers a roadmap to success in the visually dynamic and financially rewarding realm of stock media.

Chapter 8: Virtual Assistance

Navigate the landscape of remote work and discover the diverse opportunities within the realm of virtual assistance in Chapter 8 of "Unlocking Online Income" — "Virtual Assistance." This chapter serves as a comprehensive guide for individuals seeking to provide valuable support to businesses and entrepreneurs from the comfort of their own homes.

Offering Virtual Assistance Services:

The chapter kicks off by providing an in-depth exploration of the role and responsibilities of a virtual assistant (VA). Readers will gain insights into the diverse tasks Vas can undertake, from administrative duties to specialized skills like social media management, customer service, and project coordination. A roadmap is provided for those looking to carve a niche for themselves in this burgeoning field.

Platforms for Finding Clients:

Securing clients is a crucial aspect of establishing a successful virtual assistance business. This section offers practical guidance on platforms and methods for finding clients seeking virtual assistance services. Popular platforms such as Upwork, Freelancer, and specialized VA agencies are explored, providing readers with actionable tips on creating compelling profiles and crafting winning proposals to stand out in a competitive market.

Building a Successful Virtual Assistant Business:

Transitioning from freelance tasks to building a thriving virtual assistant business requires strategy and foresight. This section provides guidance on establishing and scaling a virtual assistant business, including setting competitive rates, structuring service packages, and leveraging referrals and testimonials. Real-world case studies showcase how successful Vas have positioned themselves as indispensable partners to their clients, fostering long-term relationships and consistent income.

The chapter also covers the Importance of communication skills, time management, and the ability to adapt to different industries and tasks, ensuring that virtual assistants can offer a broad range of services to meet the diverse needs of their clients.

Navigating Tools and Technology:

Efficiency is key in virtual assistance, and this section explores the essential tools and technology that can enhance a VA's productivity. From project management tools to communication platforms, readers will gain insights into the tools that streamline collaboration with clients and facilitate seamless virtual assistance services. The chapter also covers the importance of cybersecurity and data protection in the virtual assistance profession.

Networking in the Virtual Assistant Community:

Networking plays a crucial role in the success of virtual assistants. This section encourages readers to connect with other virtual assistants, join online communities, and participate in industry events. Networking not only opens doors to potential clients but also provides opportunities for skill-sharing, collaboration, and professional development.

By the end of Chapter 8, readers will have a comprehensive understanding of the virtual assistance landscape, equipped with the knowledge and tools needed to establish and grow a successful virtual assistance business. Whether exploring virtual assistance as a full-time career or a supplementary income source, this chapter provides valuable insights for individuals ready to thrive in the remote work environment

Chapter 9: Remote Consulting and Coaching

Embark on a journey into the world of professional guidance and personal development in Chapter 9 of "Unlocking Online Income" — "Remote Consulting and Coaching." This chapter is a comprehensive guide for individuals seeking to share their expertise, offer guidance, and facilitate personal growth through remote consulting and coaching services.

Providing Remote Consulting Services:

The chapter begins by delving into the realm of remote consulting, where individuals can leverage their expertise to offer specialized guidance to businesses and individuals. Readers will gain insights into the diverse fields of consulting, from business strategy and marketing to niche specialties like career counselling and financial consulting. Practical advice is provided for identifying one's unique expertise and positioning it effectively in the remote consulting landscape.

Coaching and Mentoring Online:

Building on consulting, this section explores the world of coaching and mentoring. Readers will understand the distinctions between coaching and consulting and gain insights into the methodologies and approaches that make coaching a powerful tool for personal and professional development. Real-world examples illustrate successful coaching and mentoring relationships, emphasizing the impact of positive guidance on individual growth.

Marketing Your Expertise:

A key aspect of success in remote consulting and coaching is effective marketing. This section provides a deep dive into strategic marketing techniques tailored for consultants and coaches. From creating a compelling online presence to utilizing content marketing and social media, readers will learn how to showcase their expertise and attract clients. The chapter also explores the importance of client testimonials and referrals in building a thriving consulting and coaching practice.

Developing a Successful Consulting and Coaching Business:

Transitioning from offering individual sessions to building a successful consulting or coaching business requires strategic planning. This section guides readers through essential considerations such as setting rates, structuring service packages, and managing client relationships. Case studies highlight successful consultants and coaches who have navigated challenges and achieved long-term success in their remote practices.

The chapter also covers the Importance of ongoing professional development for consultants and coaches, ensuring that they stay updated on industry trends, coaching methodologies, and best practices.

Building Client Relationships:

Effective communication and relationship-building are foundational to success in remote consulting and coaching. This section explores strategies for establishing trust with clients, creating a positive coaching environment, and managing client expectations. Practical tips on conducting virtual sessions, maintaining client confidentiality, and handling challenging situations contribute to the reader's ability to build strong and lasting client relationships.

By the end of Chapter 9, readers will possess a comprehensive understanding of the remote consulting and coaching landscape. Whether aspiring to be a business consultant, career coach, or personal development mentor, this chapter equips individuals with the knowledge and strategies needed to thrive in the rewarding and impactful world of remote consulting and coaching.

Chapter 10: Podcasting for Profit

Embark on an auditory journey into the dynamic world of digital storytelling and monetization in Chapter 10 of "Unlocking Online Income" — "Podcasting for Profit." This chapter serves as a comprehensive guide for individuals looking to turn their passion for audio content into a sustainable and lucrative online income stream.

Starting a Podcast:

The chapter begins by exploring the fundamentals of podcasting, from choosing a niche and defining your target audience to selecting the right equipment and software. Readers will gain insights into the creative and technical aspects of podcast production, ensuring a solid foundation for the journey ahead. Practical advice is provided for crafting engaging content and developing a unique podcasting style that resonates with listeners.

Monetizing Your Podcast:

While podcasting is a form of creative expression, it can also be a profitable venture. This section delves into various monetization strategies for podcasts, including sponsorships, advertising, listener donations, and premium content subscriptions. Real-world case studies illustrate how successful podcasters have strategically integrated monetization methods without compromising the integrity of their content.

Growing Your Podcast Audience:

A growing audience is the lifeblood of a successful podcast. This section provides actionable strategies for increasing listenership, including effective promotion on social media, collaboration with other podcasters, and optimizing your podcast for search engines. Listeners' feedback, reviews, and community engagement are emphasized as crucial elements in building a loyal and dedicated audience.

Podcast Marketing and Branding:

Effective marketing and branding are key to standing out in the competitive podcasting landscape. This section explores strategies for creating eye-catching podcast artwork, crafting compelling episode titles and descriptions, and leveraging social media to promote your podcast. The importance of consistent branding and a strong online presence is highlighted, ensuring that your podcast becomes a recognizable and trusted voice in your niche.

Podcasting Tools and Resources:

Podcasting involves a variety of tools and resources to streamline production and enhance the overall quality of your content. This section provides recommendations for recording and editing software, hosting platforms, and analytics tools. From episode planning to post-production, readers will gain insights into the tools that can optimize their podcasting workflow.

Navigating the Podcasting Landscape:

The podcasting landscape is ever-evolving, and this section offers insights into emerging trends and changes. From staying informed about industry updates to adapting to new technologies and audience preferences, readers will be equipped to navigate the dynamic podcasting landscape and position their shows for long-term success.

By the end of Chapter 10, readers will have a comprehensive understanding of podcasting as both a creative endeavor and a profitable online venture. Whether seeking to share stories, insights, or expertise, this chapter provides the strategies and insights needed to thrive in the immersive and rapidly growing world of podcasting for profit.

Chapter 11: Writing and Publishing E-books

Embark on a literary adventure into the realm of digital publishing with Chapter 11 of "Unlocking Online Income" — "Writing and Publishing E-books." This chapter serves as a comprehensive guide for aspiring authors and content creators seeking to transform their ideas and expertise into profitable digital publications.

Writing and Publishing Process:

The chapter begins by exploring the art of crafting compelling e-books. Readers will gain insights into the writing process, from conceptualizing ideas and outlining content to drafting and editing. Practical advice is provided for maintaining a consistent writing schedule, overcoming writer's block, and leveraging tools and software to enhance the writing process.

Choosing Your Niche and Target Audience:

Selecting the right niche and understanding your target audience are crucial steps in the e-book creation journey. This section guides readers in identifying their unique expertise and aligning it with market demand. Strategies for conducting market research, identifying reader preferences, and creating content that resonates with a specific audience are explored.

Platforms for E-book Publishing:

Dive into the diverse platforms available for publishing and distributing e-books. From self-publishing options like Kindle Direct Publishing (KDP) and Smashwords to traditional publishing routes, readers will gain insights into the pros and cons of each platform. Practical tips are provided for formatting, designing book covers, and optimizing e-book metadata to maximize visibility and sales.

Marketing Your E-book:

Creating an exceptional e-book is only part of the journey; effective marketing is essential for success. This section explores various marketing strategies, including building an author platform, utilizing social media, running promotional campaigns, and seeking reviews. Real-world case studies showcase how successful authors have strategically marketed their e-books to reach a wider audience and generate sustained sales.

Pricing Strategies and Monetization:

Setting the right price for your e-book is a critical decision that impacts both sales and profitability. This section provides insights into pricing strategies, including promotional pricing, bundling, and the use of free promotions. Readers will also explore additional monetization avenues such as audiobook adaptations, foreign translations, and licensing opportunities.

Building a Brand as an E-book Author:

Establishing a brand as an e-book author is essential for long-term success. This section explores strategies for building a personal brand, creating a professional author website, and cultivating a loyal readership. The importance of consistent branding and engagement with readers through newsletters, social media, and author events is emphasized.

Protecting Your Intellectual Property:

Understanding the legal aspects of e-book publishing is crucial for protecting intellectual property. This section provides guidance on copyright considerations, licensing options, and navigating legal challenges in the digital publishing landscape. Readers will gain insights into the importance of maintaining ownership of their work while maximizing distribution opportunities.

By the end of Chapter 11, readers will be well-equipped to embark on their journey as e-book authors, from the inception of ideas to the successful publication and marketing of their works. Whether aspiring to share fiction, non-fiction, or expertise-driven content, this chapter provides the strategies and practical insights needed to thrive in the dynamic world of writing and publishing e-books.

Chapter 12: Online Surveys and Market Research

Uncover the valuable intersection of consumer insights and online income in Chapter 12 of "Unlocking Online Income" — "Online Surveys and Market Research." This chapter serves as a comprehensive guide for individuals interested in participating in online surveys and delving into the world of market research to earn money while providing valuable feedback to businesses.

Participating in Online Surveys:

The chapter commences with an exploration of the landscape of online surveys. Readers will gain insights into the various platforms available for participating in surveys and providing feedback on products, services, and consumer preferences. Practical tips are provided for creating profiles on survey platforms, maximizing survey opportunities, and earning rewards or cash incentives for participation.

Market Research Opportunities:

Dive into the broader realm of market research, where individuals can contribute their opinions to shape the strategies of businesses and organizations. This section explores opportunities beyond surveys, including focus groups, product testing, and in-depth interviews. Readers will gain an understanding of the diverse ways in which they can engage in market research and provide valuable insights to companies seeking to improve their offerings.

Maximizing Earnings through Survey Platforms:

While participating in surveys may seem straightforward, this section offers strategies for maximizing earnings on survey platforms. Readers will learn how to identify high-paying surveys, optimize their profiles to receive targeted opportunities, and manage their time effectively to increase overall earnings. Real-world examples showcase individuals who have successfully turned online surveys into a consistent source of income.

Earning Gift Cards and Cash Rewards:

One of the primary incentives for participating in online surveys is the opportunity to earn gift cards, cash rewards, or other valuable incentives. This section explores the various reward systems employed by survey platforms and provides guidance on choosing opportunities that align with personal preferences and financial goals. Tips for redeeming rewards and managing earned incentives effectively are also covered.

Navigating the Online Survey Landscape:

The chapter goes beyond participation and delves into the dynamics of the online survey landscape. Readers will gain insights into the factors that influence survey opportunities, including demographic considerations, survey frequency, and the importance of providing honest and thoughtful responses. Strategies for avoiding scams and identifying legitimate survey opportunities contribute to a positive and rewarding experience.

Contributing to Consumer Influence:

Participating in online surveys and market research is not only about earning money but also about contributing to the influence of consumer opinions. This section explores the impact that individuals can have on product development, marketing strategies, and business decisions through their participation in surveys. Real-world examples showcase instances where consumer feedback has led to tangible changes in products and services.

By the end of Chapter 12, readers will have a comprehensive understanding of the online survey and market research landscape, equipped with the knowledge and strategies needed to participate effectively and generate income. Whether seeking to earn extra cash or contribute to the improvement of products and services, this chapter provides valuable insights for individuals ready to navigate the dynamic world of online surveys and market research.

Chapter 13: Remote Software Development and Coding

Embark on a journey into the realm of digital innovation and technology with Chapter 13 of "Unlocking Online Income" — "Remote Software Development and Coding." This chapter serves as a comprehensive guide for individuals passionate about programming and software development, providing insights into how one can thrive in the remote work landscape and turn coding skills into a lucrative online income.

Remote Work in Software Development:

The chapter opens with an exploration of the remote work landscape in the field of software development. Readers will gain insights into the advantages of remote work, including flexibility, access to a global talent pool, and the ability to work on diverse and exciting projects. Practical tips are provided for establishing a remote workspace, managing time effectively, and leveraging collaboration tools to ensure seamless communication with remote teams.

Freelancing Platforms and Job Boards:

For aspiring remote software developers, freelancing platforms and job boards are essential avenues for finding opportunities. This section delves into popular platforms like Upwork, Freelancer, and Toptal, offering guidance on creating compelling profiles, bidding on projects, and establishing a strong online presence. Real-world success stories highlight how individuals have built successful freelance careers in software development through online platforms.

Building a Portfolio and Specializing:

A robust portfolio is crucial for showcasing coding skills and attracting potential clients or employers. This section guides readers on how to build an impressive portfolio that reflects their expertise and highlights past projects. Specialization is explored as a strategy for standing out in the competitive software development landscape, allowing individuals to carve a niche in areas such as web development, mobile app development, or machine learning.

Remote Collaboration and Teamwork:

Effective collaboration is paramount in remote software development. This section explores strategies for collaborating with remote teams, leveraging version control systems, and conducting efficient code reviews. Readers will gain insights into communication tools, project management methodologies, and best practices for ensuring smooth collaboration in a remote development environment.

Creating and Selling Software Products:

Beyond freelancing, this section explores the opportunities for creating and selling software products. Readers will gain insights into the process of developing software products, including ideation, design, coding, and marketing. Real-world examples showcase individuals who have successfully brought their software products to market, generating revenue and building a brand around their creations.

Staying Current with Technology Trends:

The field of software development is dynamic, with technology trends evolving rapidly. This section emphasizes the importance of staying current with industry trends, exploring emerging technologies, and continuously enhancing coding skills. Strategies for ongoing learning, participating in online communities, and contributing to open-source projects are explored as ways to stay relevant and competitive in the ever-changing tech landscape.

By the conclusion of Chapter 13, readers will be well-equipped to navigate the landscape of remote software development and coding. Whether pursuing freelance opportunities, building software products, or contributing to collaborative projects, this chapter provides practical insights and strategies for individuals ready to thrive in the dynamic and rewarding world of remote software development.

Chapter 14: Remote Graphic Design

Embark on a visual journey into the creative and dynamic world of digital design with Chapter 14 of "Unlocking Online Income" — "Remote Graphic Design." This chapter serves as a comprehensive guide for individuals passionate about visual storytelling and design, providing insights into how one can turn graphic design skills into a lucrative online income while working remotely.

Remote Work in Graphic Design:

The chapter opens by exploring the landscape of remote work in the field of graphic design. Readers will gain insights into the advantages of working remotely, including flexibility, diverse project opportunities, and the ability to collaborate with clients globally. Practical tips are provided for creating an inspiring remote workspace, managing design projects effectively, and leveraging online tools to ensure seamless communication with clients and teams.

Freelancing Platforms and Design Communities:

For aspiring remote graphic designers, freelancing platforms and design communities play a crucial role in finding opportunities and building a client base. This section delves into popular platforms like Upwork, Fiverr, and 99designs, offering guidance on creating compelling portfolios, bidding on projects, and establishing a strong online presence. Real-world success stories highlight how designers have built successful freelance careers through online platforms and design communities.

Building a Striking Portfolio:

A standout portfolio is essential for showcasing design skills and attracting potential clients or employers. This section provides guidance on curating a visually compelling portfolio that reflects a designer's style, skills, and versatility. Strategies for presenting projects, highlighting creativity, and showcasing a diverse range of work are explored, empowering designers to make a memorable impression on prospective clients.

Specializing and Branding:

Specialization is a strategy for standing out in the competitive graphic design landscape. This section explores the benefits of specializing in specific design niches, such as logo design, branding, web design, or illustration. Readers will gain insights into the process of branding themselves as designers, creating a unique identity, and establishing a memorable brand presence in the online design community.

Effective Communication and Client Collaboration:

Successful graphic design projects hinge on effective communication and collaboration. This section provides strategies for communicating with clients remotely, understanding project requirements, and incorporating client feedback into design iterations. Real-world examples showcase how designers have navigated client relationships, ensuring client satisfaction and successful project outcomes in a remote work setting.

Creating and Selling Design Assets:

Beyond client work, this section explores opportunities for creating and selling design assets. Readers will gain insights into the process of developing design assets, such as templates, fonts, or illustrations, and selling them on platforms like Etsy, Creative Market, or their own websites. Real-world examples showcase designers who have successfully turned their creative assets into a passive income stream.

Staying Inspired and Adapting to Trends:

The field of graphic design is dynamic, with design trends evolving continuously. This section emphasizes the importance of staying inspired, exploring emerging design trends, and continuously honing design skills. Strategies for finding inspiration, participating in design communities, and adapting to changing client preferences contribute to a designer's ability to stay relevant and thrive in the ever-evolving design landscape.

By the end of Chapter 14, readers will be well-equipped to navigate the landscape of remote graphic design. Whether pursuing freelance opportunities, creating design assets, or building a personal brand, this chapter provides practical insights and strategies for individuals ready to thrive in the dynamic and visually captivating world of remote graphic design.

Chapter 15: Remote Video Editing

Embark on a visual storytelling journey and dive into the world of remote video editing with Chapter 15 of "Unlocking Online Income" — "Remote Video Editing." This chapter serves as a comprehensive guide for individuals passionate about crafting compelling video content, providing insights into how one can leverage video editing skills to earn a lucrative income while working remotely.

Remote Work in Video Editing:

The chapter begins by exploring the landscape of remote work in the field of video editing. Readers will gain insights into the benefits of working remotely, including flexibility, access to diverse projects, and collaboration with clients and teams across the globe. Practical tips are provided for creating an efficient remote workspace, managing video editing projects effectively, and leveraging online tools to ensure seamless communication with clients and collaborators.

Freelancing Platforms and Video Editing Communities:

For aspiring remote video editors, freelancing platforms and video editing communities are essential avenues for finding opportunities and building a client base. This section delves into popular platforms like Upwork, Freelancer, and Mandy, offering guidance on creating standout profiles, bidding on projects, and establishing a strong online presence. Real-world success stories highlight how video editors have built thriving freelance careers through online platforms and collaborative communities.

Building a Dynamic Video Editing Portfolio:

A dynamic portfolio is essential for showcasing video editing skills and attracting potential clients or employers. This section provides guidance on curating a compelling portfolio that reflects a video editor's style, proficiency, and versatility. Strategies for presenting showreels, highlighting different editing techniques, and showcasing a diverse range of video projects empower editors to make a memorable impression on prospective clients.

Specializing and Branding in Video Editing:

Specialization is a strategic approach to stand out in the competitive video editing landscape. This section explores the benefits of specializing in specific editing niches, such as corporate videos, documentaries, promotional content, or social media videos. Readers will gain insights into branding themselves as video editors, creating a unique identity, and establishing a memorable brand presence in the online video editing community.

Effective Communication and Collaborating Remotely:

Successful video editing projects rely on effective communication and collaboration. This section provides strategies for communicating with clients and collaborators remotely, understanding project requirements, and incorporating feedback into editing iterations. Real-world examples showcase how video editors have navigated client relationships, ensuring client satisfaction and successful project outcomes in a remote work setting.

Creating and Selling Video Assets:

Beyond client work, this section explores opportunities for creating and selling video assets. Readers will gain insights into the process of developing video assets, such as stock footage, templates, or motion graphics, and selling them on platforms like Shutterstock, VideoHive, or their own websites. Real-world examples showcase video editors who have successfully turned their creative assets into a passive income stream.

Staying Inspired and Adapting to Trends:

The field of video editing is dynamic, with editing styles and trends evolving continuously. This section emphasizes the importance of staying inspired, exploring emerging video editing trends, and continuously honing editing skills. Strategies for finding inspiration, participating in video editing communities, and adapting to changing industry preferences contribute to a video editor's ability to stay relevant and thrive in the ever-evolving visual storytelling landscape.

By the end of Chapter 15, readers will be well-equipped to navigate the landscape of remote video editing. Whether pursuing freelance opportunities, creating video assets, or building a personal brand, this chapter provides practical insights and strategies for individuals ready to thrive in the dynamic and visually captivating world of remote video editing.

Chapter 16: Virtual Real Estate: Domain Flipping

Embark on a digital real estate adventure with Chapter 16 of "Unlocking Online Income" — "Virtual Real Estate: Domain Flipping." This chapter serves as a comprehensive guide for individuals looking to navigate the virtual landscape of domain names, exploring the art of domain flipping as a means of generating a lucrative online income.

Understanding Domain Flipping:

The chapter begins by delving into the concept of domain flipping, a practice where individuals buy and sell domain names for a profit. Readers will gain insights into the fundamentals of the domain market, including factors that contribute to the value of a domain, such as keyword relevance, brandability, and market trends. Practical advice is provided for understanding the dynamics of buying and selling domains effectively.

Identifying Profitable Domains:

Success in domain flipping hinges on the ability to identify valuable and potentially lucrative domain names. This section provides strategies for researching market trends, using keyword tools, and staying informed about industry developments to spot opportunities. Real-world examples showcase how domain flippers have successfully identified and acquired domains that later became in-demand assets.

Registering and Acquiring Domains:

Navigating the process of registering and acquiring domains is a crucial aspect of domain flipping. Readers will gain insights into selecting reputable domain registrars, understanding the domain registration process, and negotiating domain purchases. Strategies for bidding on expired domains, participating in domain auctions, and negotiating with domain owners contribute to a comprehensive understanding of the domain acquisition process.

Valuing and Pricing Domains:

Assigning the right value to a domain is essential for successful flipping. This section explores methods for valuing domains, considering factors such as search engine optimization (SEO) potential, brandability, and market demand. Strategies for pricing domains competitively, negotiating with potential buyers, and maximizing profitability are covered, offering readers a roadmap for effective domain valuation.

Selling Domains Effectively:

Successfully selling domains requires effective marketing and negotiation skills. This section guides readers on creating compelling domain listings, utilizing domain marketplaces, and leveraging social media and other channels for promotion. Real-world case studies illustrate successful domain sales strategies, emphasizing the importance of clear communication and building trust with potential buyers.

Mitigating Risks and Legal Considerations:

The domain flipping landscape comes with its own set of risks and legal considerations. This section provides guidance on mitigating risks, avoiding domain disputes, and understanding trademark laws related to domain names. Readers will gain insights into the importance of conducting due diligence, respecting intellectual property rights, and navigating potential legal challenges in the domain flipping business.

Building a Domain Flipping Business:

Transitioning from individual flips to building a sustainable domain flipping business requires strategic planning. This section explores considerations such as portfolio management, reinvesting profits, and scaling operations. Readers will gain insights into creating a brand for their domain flipping business, establishing an online presence, and developing a reputation in the domain flipping community.

Staying Informed and Adapting to Trends:

The domain market is dynamic, with trends and preferences evolving over time. This section emphasizes the importance of staying informed about industry trends, emerging technologies, and market demands. Strategies for adapting to changes in the domain landscape, diversifying domain portfolios, and continuously learning about the virtual real estate market contribute to long-term success in domain flipping.

By the end of Chapter 16, readers will be well-equipped to venture into the world of virtual real estate through domain flipping. Whether pursuing domain flipping as a side hustle or a full-time business, this chapter provides practical insights and strategies for individuals ready to unlock online income through the art of acquiring, valuing, and selling domain names.

Chapter 17: Online Stock Trading and Investments

Embark on a journey into the dynamic world of financial markets and wealth creation with Chapter 17 of "Unlocking Online Income" — "Online Stock Trading and Investments." This chapter serves as a comprehensive guide for individuals seeking to navigate the intricacies of online stock trading, exploring the opportunities and strategies for building wealth through intelligent investment decisions.

Understanding Online Stock Trading:

The chapter begins by providing a foundational understanding of online stock trading, introducing readers to the basics of financial markets, stocks, and investment instruments. From stock exchanges to trading platforms, readers will gain insights into the infrastructure that facilitates online stock trading.

Creating an Investment Strategy:

Successful stock trading requires a well-thought-out investment strategy. This section guides readers through the process of creating a personalized investment strategy based on factors such as risk tolerance, financial goals, and time horizon. Strategies for asset allocation, diversification, and goal-specific investing are explored to empower readers in making informed and strategic investment decisions.

Choosing an Online Brokerage Platform:

Navigating the online stock market begins with choosing the right brokerage platform. This section delves into considerations for selecting an online brokerage, including fees, account types, research tools, and user interface. Real-world comparisons and reviews of popular online brokerages provide readers with the information needed to make an informed choice.

Fundamental and Technical Analysis:

Understanding how to analyse stocks is fundamental to successful trading. This section explores both fundamental and technical analysis, providing readers with the tools to evaluate a company's financial health, growth potential, and market trends. Real-world examples illustrate how investors use these analyses to make informed decisions about buying or selling stocks.

Risk Management and Portfolio Diversification:

Managing risks is a critical aspect of online stock trading. This section emphasizes the importance of risk management strategies, including setting stop-loss orders, position sizing, and understanding market volatility. Readers will also gain insights into the concept of portfolio diversification and how it can mitigate risks associated with individual stock investments.

Trading Strategies and Styles:

Explore various trading strategies and styles, from day trading and swing trading to long-term investing and value investing. This section provides insights into the characteristics of each strategy, helping readers identify the approach that aligns with their goals and risk tolerance. Real-world examples showcase successful investors who have employed different strategies to build wealth over time.

Staying Informed and Continuous Learning:

The financial markets are dynamic and ever-changing. This section emphasizes the importance of staying informed about market news, economic indicators, and global events that can impact investments. Strategies for continuous learning, utilizing financial news sources, and staying updated on investment trends contribute to a reader's ability to adapt to the evolving landscape of online stock trading.

Tax Considerations and Regulations:

Understanding tax implications is crucial for maximizing investment returns. This section provides guidance on tax considerations related to stock trading, including capital gains, dividends, and tax-efficient investment strategies. Readers will also gain insights into regulatory aspects, ensuring compliance with relevant financial regulations and standards.

Building Wealth for the Long Term:

The ultimate goal of online stock trading is often long-term wealth creation. This section explores strategies for building wealth over time, including dollar-cost averaging, reinvesting dividends, and the power of compounding. Real-world success stories highlight individuals who have built substantial wealth through disciplined and strategic long-term investing.

By the conclusion of Chapter 17, readers will be well-equipped to embark on their journey into the world of online stock trading and investments. Whether seeking to generate additional income, build a retirement fund, or grow long-term wealth, this chapter provides practical insights and strategies for individuals ready to unlock the potential of the financial markets.

Chapter 18: Remote Fitness Coaching

Embark on a journey into the world of virtual fitness and wellness with Chapter 18 of "Unlocking Online Income" — "Remote Fitness Coaching." This chapter serves as a comprehensive guide for individuals passionate about health and fitness, providing insights into how one can turn fitness expertise into a fulfilling and lucrative online coaching business.

Understanding Remote Fitness Coaching:

The chapter begins by exploring the concept of remote fitness coaching, where fitness professionals leverage online platforms to deliver personalized training, guidance, and support to clients. Readers will gain insights into the benefits of remote coaching, including accessibility, flexibility, and the ability to reach a global audience.

Establishing Your Fitness Coaching Niche:

Identifying a niche is crucial for success in the competitive fitness coaching landscape. This section guides readers in defining their unique fitness coaching niche, whether it's strength training, weight loss, athletic performance, or specialized programs like yoga or prenatal fitness. Strategies for aligning expertise with market demand and standing out in the online fitness community are explored.

Building an Online Presence:

Creating a strong online presence is fundamental to attracting clients and establishing credibility. This section provides guidance on creating a professional website, utilizing social media, and leveraging content marketing to showcase expertise and connect with potential clients.

Real-world examples illustrate how successful fitness coaches have built a brand and attracted a dedicated online following.

Online Coaching Platforms and Tools:

Navigating the landscape of online coaching platforms is essential for remote fitness coaches. This section explores popular platforms and tools, such as Trainerize, Zoom, and specialized fitness apps, providing insights into their features and functionalities. Practical advice is offered on selecting the right tools to streamline communication, program delivery, and client engagement.

Creating Customized Fitness Programs:

Tailoring fitness programs to individual client needs is a cornerstone of effective coaching. This section guides readers on the process of assessing client goals, creating personalized workout plans, and adapting programs based on client progress and feedback. Strategies for integrating nutritional guidance and lifestyle recommendations into coaching services are explored.

Client Communication and Motivation:

Effective communication is key to successful coaching relationships. This section provides insights into building rapport with clients, conducting virtual consultations, and maintaining regular communication. Strategies for keeping clients motivated, accountable, and engaged in their fitness journey are covered, emphasizing the importance of a supportive and encouraging coaching approach.

Marketing and Attracting Clients:

Building a client base requires strategic marketing efforts. This section explores marketing strategies tailored for fitness coaches, including social media marketing, online advertising, and collaboration with influencers. Real-world examples showcase successful marketing campaigns that have helped fitness coaches reach a wider audience and attract clients from diverse backgrounds.

Setting Prices and Managing Finances:

Determining pricing structures and managing finances are critical aspects of running a successful fitness coaching business. This section provides guidance on setting competitive rates, structuring service packages, and implementing secure payment methods. Strategies for managing business expenses, tracking income, and planning for growth contribute to the financial sustainability of a remote fitness coaching business.

Continuous Learning and Professional Development:

The fitness industry evolves, and staying current with trends and research is essential for effective coaching. This section emphasizes the importance of continuous learning and professional development, whether through certifications, workshops, or staying informed about the latest fitness innovations. Real-world examples showcase coaches who have prioritized ongoing education to enhance their coaching skills. By the end of Chapter 18, readers will be well-equipped to embark on their journey as remote fitness coaches, from defining their niche and building an online presence to delivering personalized programs and attracting a dedicated clientele. Whether pursuing fitness coaching as a full-time career or a supplementary income source, this chapter provides practical insights and strategies for individuals ready to thrive in the dynamic world of remote fitness coaching.

Chapter 19: Online Language Tutoring

Embark on a linguistic journey into the realm of virtual language education with Chapter 19 of "Unlocking Online Income" — "Online Language Tutoring." This chapter serves as a comprehensive guide for individuals proficient in languages, providing insights into how one can transform language expertise into a rewarding and profitable online tutoring business.

Understanding Online Language Tutoring:

The chapter begins by exploring the landscape of online language tutoring, where language enthusiasts leverage digital platforms to teach and mentor learners across the globe. Readers will gain insights into the advantages of online language tutoring, including accessibility, cultural exchange, and the ability to connect with a diverse student base.

Choosing Your Language Specialization:

Identifying a language specialization is crucial for success in online language tutoring. This section guides readers in determining the languages they are proficient in and passionate about teaching. Strategies for aligning language expertise with market demand, considering target audiences, and standing out in the online language education community are explored.

Building an Online Tutoring Profile:

Creating a compelling online tutoring profile is fundamental to attracting students. This section provides guidance on selecting reputable tutoring platforms, creating a professional profile, and showcasing language proficiency and teaching experience. Real-world examples illustrate how successful language tutors have built a strong online presence and attracted a dedicated student base.

Leveraging Online Language Learning Platforms:

Navigating the landscape of online language learning platforms is essential for language tutors. This section explores popular platforms such as iTalki, Preply, and Verbling, providing insights into their features, policies, and community dynamics. Practical advice is offered on creating an engaging profile, setting competitive rates, and utilizing platform resources to enhance the tutoring experience.

Designing Effective Language Lessons:

Crafting effective language lessons is key to successful tutoring. This section guides readers on the process of planning and structuring lessons, incorporating language skills (listening, speaking, reading, writing), and adapting lessons to individual student needs. Strategies for addressing common challenges, such as language proficiency levels and diverse learning styles, are explored.

Building a Positive Tutor-Student Relationship:

Establishing a positive relationship with students is essential for effective language tutoring. This section provides insights into communication strategies, creating a supportive learning environment, and addressing student concerns. Real-world examples showcase how successful language tutors have fostered strong connections with their students, contributing to positive learning outcomes.

Marketing and Attracting Students:

Building a student base requires strategic marketing efforts. This section explores marketing strategies tailored for language tutors, including social media marketing, online advertising, and creating instructional content. Real-world examples showcase successful marketing campaigns that have helped tutors reach a wider audience and attract students interested in language learning.

Setting Prices and Managing Finances:

Determining pricing structures and managing finances are critical aspects of running a successful language tutoring business. This section provides guidance on setting competitive rates, structuring lesson packages, and implementing secure payment methods. Strategies for managing business expenses, tracking income, and planning for growth contribute to the financial sustainability of an online language tutoring business.

Continuous Learning and Professional Development:

Language learning is a lifelong journey, and staying informed about language trends and teaching methodologies is essential for effective tutoring. This section emphasizes the importance of continuous learning and professional development, whether through language courses, attending workshops, or staying updated on the latest language education innovations. Real-world examples showcase tutors who have prioritized ongoing education to enhance their teaching skills.

By the end of Chapter 19, readers will be well-equipped to embark on their journey as online language tutors, from defining their language specialization and building an online presence to delivering effective lessons and attracting a dedicated student base. Whether pursuing language tutoring as a full-time career or a supplementary income source, this chapter provides practical insights and strategies for individuals ready to thrive in the dynamic world of online language education.

Chapter 20: The Future of Online Income

Embark on a visionary exploration into the evolving landscape of online income with Chapter 20 of "Unlocking Online Income" — "The Future of Online Income." This concluding chapter serves as a guide to understanding the trends, technologies, and opportunities that are shaping the future of earning a living in the digital realm.

Emerging Trends in the Digital Economy:

The chapter begins by delving into the emerging trends that are transforming the digital economy. Readers will gain insights into the impact of artificial intelligence, blockchain technology, remote work, and evolving consumer behaviours on the ways individuals can generate income online. The exploration extends to the gig economy, digital currencies, and the integration of cutting-edge technologies into various online income streams.

Technological Innovations Shaping Online Income:

As technology continues to advance, this section provides an in-depth look at the innovations that are reshaping the online income landscape. From the rise of virtual reality (VR) and augmented reality (AR) in online experiences to the potential of 5G connectivity in enabling faster and more immersive digital interactions, readers will be introduced to the technological advancements that are set to redefine how individuals work and earn online.

The Influence of Remote Work on Online Income:

The paradigm shift towards remote work is explored in this section, emphasizing its profound impact on how individuals earn income online. Readers will gain insights into the evolving nature of remote work, the tools and platforms facilitating virtual collaboration, and the growing acceptance of remote work arrangements by businesses worldwide. Strategies for adapting to remote work trends and capitalizing on the opportunities it presents are discussed.

Evolving E-Commerce and Digital Marketplaces:

The future of online income is closely tied to the evolution of e-commerce and digital marketplaces. This section examines the trends in online shopping behaviors, the integration of artificial intelligence in personalized shopping experiences, and the growth of niche markets. Readers will gain insights into how entrepreneurs and freelancers can position themselves to thrive in the dynamic world of digital commerce.

Personal Branding and Building Online Communities:

Building a personal brand and fostering online communities play a pivotal role in the future of online income. This section explores the importance of personal branding, the use of social media, and the cultivation of engaged communities around niche interests. Real-world examples showcase individuals who have successfully monetized their personal brand and leveraged online communities to generate sustainable income.

Financial Technologies (FinTech) and Digital Currencies:

The chapter delves into the role of financial technologies (FinTech) and digital currencies in shaping the future of online income. Readers will gain insights into the impact of blockchain technology on financial transactions, the rise of cryptocurrencies, and the potential integration of decentralized finance (DeFi) in online income streams. Strategies for navigating the evolving landscape of digital finance are explored.

The Importance of Continuous Learning:

In the fast-paced digital era, continuous learning is emphasized as a key factor for success in generating online income. This section provides guidance on staying informed about industry trends, acquiring new skills, and adapting to evolving technologies. Strategies for pursuing online courses, participating in online communities, and embracing a growth mindset are discussed.

Navigating Challenges and Seizing Opportunities:

The future of online income comes with its own set of challenges and opportunities. This section provides insights into potential obstacles such as increased competition, changing algorithms, and cybersecurity risks. Strategies for navigating challenges and seizing emerging opportunities, whether through diversification, innovation, or strategic partnerships, are discussed.

Sustainable and Ethical Online Income Practices:

As the digital economy evolves, the importance of sustainability and ethical practices in online income generation becomes increasingly significant. This section explores the trends towards conscious consumerism, ethical business practices, and the role of social and environmental responsibility in shaping the future of online income. Strategies for aligning online income pursuits with sustainable and ethical principles are discussed.

By the conclusion of Chapter 20, readers will have a forward-looking perspective on the future of online income. Whether navigating technological advancements, adapting to changing work dynamics, or embracing emerging opportunities, this chapter provides insights and strategies for individuals ready to thrive in the dynamic and evolving landscape of earning a living online.

Conclusion

As we close the pages of "Unlocking Online Income," our journey through the vast and dynamic landscape of the digital frontier comes to an end. This book has been a comprehensive guide, unveiling the myriad opportunities available to individuals seeking to harness the power of the internet to generate income. From the gig economy and remote work to diverse online ventures, we've explored the diverse pathways leading to financial success in the digital age.

The digital era has not only reshaped the way we work but has also democratized income generation, offering a wealth of opportunities for those with the vision and determination to seize them. Our exploration has taken us through a multitude of online avenues, from freelancing and entrepreneurship to investing and coaching, each presenting a unique tapestry of possibilities.

In the gig economy, we've witnessed the rise of flexible work arrangements and the empowerment of freelancers across the globe. Remote work has become a cornerstone of the modern workforce, breaking down geographical barriers and opening up a world of opportunities for those seeking location-independent careers. Entrepreneurs have found fertile ground in the digital realm, with e-commerce, blogging, and podcasting offering avenues for creative expression and financial success.

The chapters on Investing and trading have shed light on the potential of financial markets, providing insights into the strategies and tools needed to navigate the complexities of online investment. Meanwhile, coaching and tutoring have emerged as platforms for sharing expertise and making a positive impact on others' lives, while also generating income.

As we've journeyed through the diverse chapters of this book, certain themes have emerged as crucial pillars of success in the online arena. Adaptability, continuous learning, and embracing technological advancements have proven to be key components in staying relevant and thriving in the ever-evolving digital landscape. Whether you are a freelancer, entrepreneur, investor, or coach, the ability to pivot, upskill, and embrace change is paramount.

The future of online Income holds promises and challenges, shaped by emerging technologies, remote work trends, and evolving consumer behaviors. As we peer into the horizon of the digital frontier, the importance of sustainable and ethical practices becomes apparent. A conscientious approach to online income generation, one that considers the impact on society and the environment, is not just a choice but a responsibility.

In conclusion, "Unlocking Online Income" has been a guidebook for those ready to embark on a journey into the digital frontier. It is a testament to the vast opportunities that exist for individuals willing to explore, innovate, and adapt. Whether you're looking to diversify your income streams, launch a new career, or simply explore the potential of the online world, the insights and strategies presented in this book are designed to empower you on your journey.

As you step forward into the digital frontier, may you find fulfillment, success, and a wealth of experiences in the world of online income. Remember, the internet is not just a tool; it's a vast landscape waiting to be explored, and your potential within it is boundless. Here's to unlocking new horizons and realizing the full potential of your online endeavors. Safe travels, and may your journey be as rewarding as the destination.

About the Author

Jatin Sharma, a dynamic innovator in the digital realm, brings a wealth of expertise to "Unlocking Online Income." A versatile professional with a passion for history , Jatin has successfully navigated the ever-changing landscape of the digital age. Known for achievements, his commitment to continuous learning and ethical practices sets the tone for a guide that empowers readers to thrive in online endeavors. Connect with Jatin on [social media handles] to stay updated on his insights and contributions in the ever-evolving world of online opportunity.

Also by Jatin Sharma

Crafting The Iconic Taj Mahal
Unlocking Online Income